Living Like a King

A plea and a plan for the simple life

by
Edward W. O'Rourke
Bishop of Peoria

TEMPLEGATE PUBLISHERS
Springfield, Illinois

ISBN: 87243-087-1

Published by
Templegate Publishers
302 East Adams Street
Springfield, Illinois 62701

Table of Contents

Introduction

"Living Like a King" can be understood as living luxuriously in a world of needful people. This book is a protest against such a life style. On the other hand, living soberly and justly in accord with the word and example of Christ the King is precisely the ideal urged in these reflections.

This is a plea for moderation in our use of goods and services, as well as a plea to greatly reduce our consumption of luxuries — fuel-guzzling automobiles; non-essential household appliances; extravagant expenditures on recreation and vacations; large, fashion-directed wardrobes; rich, highly processed foods and palatial homes. I also question the place in a rational life style for tobacco, alcoholic beverages, gambling and drugs.

I recommend instead that we seek a joyful, rewarding life, our joys and fulfillment coming from loving exchanges with family and friends, from religion, music and art, from our work, hobbies and other activities which are truly uplifting and whose rewards are enduring.

This little book is a protest against avarice, worship of bigness, preoccupation with material things, exaggerated use of artifical foods, and against all neglect of the poor, all exploitation of people.[1]

The undisciplined consumption of energy and other limited resources by the people of the United States is one of the chief causes of inflation and trade deficits. Even though these problems are a serious threat to our economic stability and to world order, we seem unwilling to cope with them. Even a modest reduction in consumption would reduce these problems to manageable proportions.

For the Christian, the most moving reasons for a simple life style are the example and teachings of Christ. He is the King we must follow and whose life we are urged to imitate. Living like this king: that is our high calling. The first thing required of the Christian is that he love God and neighbor. John the Apostle in his first Epistle (3,17) argues: "I ask you, how can God's love survive in a man who has enough of this world's goods yet closes his heart to his brother when he sees him in need? Little children, let us love in deed and in truth and not merely talk about it."

A simple life style is not a panacea. Issues so vast as ecology, world poverty and social justice cannot be resolved with a single simple remedy. On the other hand, if a substantial number of people were to reduce their consumption of goods and services by even ten percent, the beneficial effects would be enormous.

The views contained in this book are offered in the realization that they contradict many values and practices prevalent in the United States today. But a simple life style is, perhaps, an idea whose time has come. During the past generation many Americans have diligently sought happiness and fulfillment from this country's material abundance, from the gadgets and pleasures offered by modern industry and technology. We now realize that such a quest is futile.

Thus disillusioned by an unsatisfactory excursion into the "paradise" of materialism, haunted by the realization that we are treating the world's poor and powerless unjustly, finding that we are polluting planet earth dangerously, sensing that there is a great dichotomy between our religious profession and our religious practice — perhaps now we will see that it is time to take a bold step toward a life style which is satisfying, ecologically acceptable, consistent with the demands of social justice, and in keeping with our religious ideals.

Chapter I:
Justice and Sobriety
on Planet Earth

The journeys of the astronauts to the moon have given all of us a new understanding and appreciation of the earth as a unique haven of the living. When Alan Shepard stepped out on the moon's surface on February 5, 1971 he remarked: "It certainly is a stark place here at Fra Mauro." When he looked back toward the earth he saw it was green, blue and beautiful, contrasting sharply with the blackness of space behind it.

Evidence now at our disposal suggests that there is no life on the moon, and probably no life on any of the planets in the solar system other than earth. Life is, in fact, such an extraordinary and improbable phenomenon that it may be a relatively rare occurrence anywhere in the universe. The earth is able to sustain life because of its distance from the sun, its water, its absence of poisonous gases, the presence of oxygen, and the degree at which its axis tilts. As we look at the pictures of the earth as seen from the moon we are drawn to the conclusion that the earth is truly unique, a home for living beings. Life is complex, wonderful and precious. We never cease to wonder at the beauty of living things and at their ability to grow and flourish. In the case of human beings, we marvel at the ability to move purposefully, to understand, communicate and love.

Now we are faced with an environmental crisis, which has prompted an increasing number of our nation's leaders to worry publicly about the future of our environment — we are urged to muster both private and governmental resources to remedy our environmental problems. The reminders offered us by ecologists that nature is a unity and that mankind is very much a part of it are especially timely today. Air, water, minerals, sunlight, plants, animals and human beings are inter-dependent in a beautiful, complex and marvelous ecological system. When the proper interaction among these creatures is maintained, nature regenerates itself. One species' wastes become the other species' support, and the decaying remains of one generation of plants and animals become the nourishment of the next generation. From a study of ecology we can learn that one of the fundamental causes of our environmental crisis is our habit of resorting to unprincipled, short-range, expedient methods for accomplishing material, selfish goals. It shows us the folly of disregarding the laws of nature and the delicate inter-relationships between human beings and nature.

Love for gadgets, and the consequent dependence on technology and urbanization have helped cause our waste and pollution of the earth's resources, marring the beauty of our planet and impairing its functions. The air we breathe is filled with noxious gases; our water supply is polluted with human and industrial wastes. On every side we are harassed by litter, garbage and noise. Dead birds on our lawns and dead fishes on the banks of our lakes and streams remind us that we have been very poor stewards of the good earth which God has placed in our care. They also suggest that we may destroy ourselves if pollution of our environment goes on much longer.

Our responsible, intelligent dominion over nature requires that we use its resources sparingly. Whenever possible we should recycle natural resources so they can be used again and again; nature itself does this. Nature has a marvelous capacity to renew itself. With proper stewardship on our part, our farms, forests, waterways and most of our resources can become increasingly more productive and more beautiful.

We the people of the United States are the world's most irresponsible polluters. In order to remedy this situation, we must readjust our attitudes and values. Material, quantitative goals have dominated our strivings as individuals and as a nation. Now we must begin to place less stress on our gross national product, and give more attention to the quality of life which results from the choices we make. We have a standard of living so luxurious that it can be maintained only by exploiting resources needed by future generations and, in some instances, by exploiting people of other nations. It is time to assume a more sober and equitable posture among the people and the natural resources of the world.

Although the people of the United States constitute only six percent of the world's population, they consume about forty percent of the world's goods and services, and many of these require for their production the extensive use of energy and other limited resources. This fact is necessarily a challenge to the rights of the people of other nations, who are being denied a fair share of the resources of our planet.

These statistics are even more disturbing if we translate them into the stark contrasts which exist between the life-style of Americans and that of people in the Third World. While most Third World people suffer from malnutrition, over half of the people in America are at least ten percent above their ideal weight. A typical Third World family lives in a one-room hut; a typical American family has ten times that living space. Walking, bicycling and riding burros are typical means of transportation in the Third World; most American families have at least one auto. Television sets, kitchen appliances and other gadgets we consider essential have never been used by most Third World families.

It is equally obvious that to the extent that we live extravagantly we limit our ability to aid our less fortunate fellow-men. Such a policy is neither rational nor humane.

I would propose a simpler way of life by using natural resources more responsibly; ending the pollution of our environment; and respecting the rights of our fellow men to life's essentials. In other words, our motives for such a life should include stewardship of resources, ecological consideration, and the demands of social justice.

Conversely, the style of life to which I object includes a preoccupation with material possessions, and a proliferation of gadgets which consume excessive energy in their operation and cause pollution in their production. Not only does such a life-style waste resources and pollute our environment; it usually fails to meet the esthetic needs of people. It involves an endless quest of more and more possessions until satiety takes over.

The way of life I propose calls for the use of materials as a means to embellish, not replace our spiritual, artistic and cultural activities. I hope that more specific details of this life which I recommend will emerge in the next two chapters.

Chapter II:
Using Good Things Moderately

F ood, clothing, shelter, transportation, recreation and medical care are essential for the well-being of all people. Extravagant use of these essentials in a hungry, needful world is obscene: we should observe moderation even in the use of good things. Our individual needs should be pursued in a manner compatible with the needs of others and with environmental consideration, and our choices should be made with reference to a balanced appreciation of values. We should stress quality as well as quantity, esthetic as well as practical considerations.

While nearly half of the human race suffers from malnutrition, obesity is a major health hazard in the United States. Here, over half of the population weigh at least ten percent above their ideal weight; and twenty-five percent of adult men and thirty-three percent of adult women in this nation are twenty percent above their ideal weight.[2]

A rational life style must involve less food consumption. It also calls for a reduction in the degree of refinement of our foods, and in the use of food additives. Sugar, white bleached flour, soft drinks and various sweetened and

salted foods add calories and few useful
nutrients to our diet. They are a partial cause of
obesity, tooth decay, high blood-pressure and
heart disease. They are also costly. Less refined,
more nearly natural foods (such as fruits,
vegetables, lean meat, fish, whole wheat and
dairy products) are economical features of a
balanced diet.

Excessive advertising and packaging of foods
also bring about negative ecological and
economic results. Much food packaging is done
in plastics, which are derived from petroleum, a
limited natural resource in increasingly
short supply.

Gardening is an excellent means of
producing high quality vegetables and foods at
minimal costs; food budgets can also be
stretched by buying directly from food
producers, through farmers' markets and
producers' cooperatives.

We must also question the propriety of
Americans' spending nearly three billion dollars
a year on pet foods in a world where most of
our fellow human beings lack sufficient food. In
most instances prepared baby food is more
costly, and less healthful, than the foods which
mothers can prepare from ordinary groceries.
Cooking and crushing vegetables and fruits for
the baby is a significantly more economical
method than buying the same foods in jars
or cans.[3]

Surely, we Americans could greatly improve
our health and reduce our expenditure for food
if we were more discerning about where we buy

our groceries, what we eat, and how we prepare our food.

Our use of clothing is also wasteful. Pressured by advertisers and influenced by peers, many Americans buy clothing which they do not need and accept styles which are uncomfortable and costly. For ecological reasons as well as for comfort, we should consider a more extensive use of natural fabrics, such as wool, cotton and linen. Wool is warm and long-wearing, cotton comfortable and absorbent, and linen is heat resistant and durable. These fabrics are derived from animals and plants, which are renewable resources. On the other hand, most synthetic fibers are derived from petroleum, an exhaustible resource. Making and mending your own clothing is an obvious way to reduce your clothing budget; and of course, many persons find sewing a satisfying and creative hobby.

Energy shortages are occasioning significant changes in the size and construction of our homes. More extensive use of insulation and more efficient approaches to heating and cooling are means of reducing energy costs. In many parts of our nation solar energy could be utilized as an economical means of supplying at least a part of the energy required in our homes.

American extravagance is most conspicuous in our choice of transportation. An automobile consumes two and one-fourth times as much energy per passenger mile as does a bus. Obviously, much greater economy results when we turn from automobile transportation to bicycling. The typical automobile contains 3,500 pounds of steel; a bicycle about 25 pounds. Automobiles are the greatest single cause of air pollution in our nation. It is fairly obvious, then, that a rational life style must include less use of automobiles, more car pooling, more use of public transportation, more bicycling and more walking.

A simple life style calls for less purchasing of recreation and more do-it-yourself recreations. Creating your own music, sharing a sport or game with a friend, a walk in the park, reading a good book — these are inexpensive and generally satisfying forms of recreation. Exercise is commendable, but most exercise gadgets are of little or no value. Many commercialized recreations exhaust and irritate us, rather than add to our joy and well-being.

No rational person will deliberately neglect essential medical care. On the other hand, many of the non-prescription medications consumed by Americans are either harmful to the health or ineffective. Our use of food, clothing, shelter, transportation, recreation and medical care should, if it is wise, advance our well-being and reduce our expenditures. The key to this is a combination of moderation and discernment. For most of us a return to natural foods and fabrics, more carefully planned housing and heating, reduced use of automobiles, more creative recreation, and a substantially reduced use of medications, would greatly improve our life styles.

Chapter III:
Costly "Vices"

In Chapter I, we considered the moderate use of food, clothing, shelter, and other things, which are both good and essential for a person's well-being. In this chapter we will look at those things which are *not* essential, such as tobacco, alcohol, gambling and drugs. I refer to them as "vices," not because they are incapable of a correct use, but because they are inherently dangerous, and for many people prove hurtful. In all cases, nevertheless, they are costly, and we should question the inclusion of these costly "vices" in our way of living.

One of the more questionable contributions of the American Indian to his European brothers is tobacco and the practice of ingesting its smoke. There is a very large body of evidence which forces us to conclude that cigarette smoking is a major cause of emphysema, heart disease and lung cancer. More than eight out of ten fires are caused by smoking material and matches discarded by careless smokers. During 1976, people in the United States spent $15.7 billion for tobacco. In addition we spent $27.5 billion for tobacco-related health care, lost production and fire losses.[4] Young people particularly should not shackle themselves with this costly, unhealthful practice.

Alcoholic beverages taken in moderation at meals are not seriously hurtful to health. Approximately 70 percent of the adults of our nation drink such beverages occasionally. On the other hand, the way many Americans use alcoholic beverages is both unhealthful and addictive. Americans spend approximately $32 billion per year on alcoholic beverages. This, however, is a relatively small part of the price we pay for our use of alcohol. Ten percent of Americans who drink are alcoholic. The cost of alcoholism in terms of lost earnings, ill health and human misery is staggering. Half of all homicides and auto accidents are caused by persons who have been drinking.

The estimated cost of alcoholism to our nation in 1975 was $42,750,000,000. (This estimate is based on a study prepared for the National Institute on Alcohol Abuse and Alcoholism by researchers Berry, Boland, Smart and Kovak.) The following are the major alcohol-related expenses:

Lost Production	$19,640,000,000
Health and Medical	12,740,000,000
Motor Vehicle Accidents	5,140,000,000
Violent Crime	2,860,000,000
Social Response	1,940,000,000
Fire Losses	430,000,000
Total	$42,750,000,000[5]

Surely, then, a rational life style must include either no use of alcohol or at most a very temperate use of this dangerous chemical.

It is almost a truism to state that drug abuse is a costly and dangerous practice. It is hard to imagine a situation in which the use of hallucinatory drugs can be justified. A rational person will, of course, want to stay in touch with the real world, rather than seek escape in the use of such drugs. Similarly, narcotics such as cocaine and heroin may lessen pain for a time, but result in a vastly greater distress when their effects have worn off. A further tragic implication of drug abuse is the extent to which criminals are involved in the distribution and sale of such drugs. Drug addicts, in turn, consistently resort to stealing to support their costly habit.

The Office of Drug Enforcement Administration, Washington, D.C., estimates the annual purchase cost of heroin, cocaine and other illicit substances at $20 billion.[6] The National Institute on Drug Abuse estimates the annual medical and social costs of drug abuse to our nation at $10,338,000,000. The major items in this estimate are: unemployability — $2,478,000,000; absenteeism — $1,594,000,000; incarceration — $1,205,000,000; law enforcement — $1,342,000,000; nondrug crime — $1,334,000,000; drug abuse prevention — $995,000,000; and medical treatment — $610,400,000.

The life style I am proposing, obviously, is diametrically opposed to that reflected in the comtemporary drug culture.

Taking a chance is a normal part of living. Many occupations and undertakings are rewarding precisely because they involve risk. On the other hand, those who patronize organized gambling establishments are not really taking a chance. They are almost certain to lose, particularly if they engage in such gambling frequently. United States citizens spend approximately $40 billion per year on gambling.[7] Moreover, the Mafia and other criminal syndicates have a significant degree of control over the gambling industry in this nation; and each year they gross $2 billion from their gambling enterprises. If we patronize them, we are increasing this threat to our nation's security. A rational life style can certainly include risks for a higher purpose, but it has little place for gambling, with its encouragement of the vain hope for a quick and easy profit.

The four "vices" described above cost the people of this nation approximately $190.28 billion in 1976. According to the U.S. Department of Health, Education and Welfare, during 1976-77 our total expenditures for education — elementary, secondary and higher — was $142.3 billion. This represents a severe indictment of our life style.

Experience shows that declaiming against these "vices" has little effect upon the hold they have on people. We must propose alternative activities which will be more attractive than these hazardous ones. Christians will find real alternatives in the practice of their religion and we will say more about this in following chapters, and will in addition offer some concrete suggestions.

Chapter IV:
Life Style For
Christians

The style of life recommended in previous chapters could be defended from merely humanistic principles. It is a way of life required by right reason and human decency.

When we propose a life style in the light of Christian beliefs and ideals, we must see that there are additional motives for embracing it, reasons which have to do with the nature of Christianity itself.

Those who live luxurious, materialistic and wasteful lives can draw little consolation from the life and teachings of Christ. Jesus' way of life was simple almost to the point of austerity. He was born in a stable, laid in a manager and wrapped with swaddling clothes. His life at Nazareth was certainly laborious and bereft of most luxuries. During his public life, Jesus declared: "The foxes have their lairs, the birds in the sky have nests, but the Son of Man has nowhere to lay his head." (Matthew 8, 20) He died on a cross, stripped of his garments, and was buried in another man's grave.

On the other hand, Jesus did not hesitate to join in weddings and other festivities. He was not nearly so severe as the Pharisees in His interpretation of the Sabbath rest and laws regarding fasting. Jesus appreciated beauty in nature, in the temple at Jerusalem, and in the people about him. His example suggests that luxury is unbecoming, but that beauty is needed by all people.

The gospel message is replete with harsh words for the wealthy, and with support for those who are poor. In the gospel according to St. Luke we read: "But woe to you rich, for your consolation is now." (6, 24) Even more telling is the parable of the rich man and Lazarus. The rich man not only lived luxuriously; he was callously insensitive to the suffering of Lazarus. His punishment was eternal damnation. (Luke 16, 19-31) There is an obvious parallel between this parable and affluent individuals and nations who are little concerned with the abject poverty of millions of their fellow human beings. Jesus consistently manifested a special love and concern for the poor, the heartbroken and the ill. He identifies himself with the messiah described by Isaiah: "The spirit of the Lord is upon me; therefore, He has anointed me. He has sent me to bring glad tidings to the poor, to proclaim liberty to captives, recovery of sight to the blind and release to prisoners . . ." (Isaiah 6, 1-2; Luke 4, 16-18) Jesus counsels the Pharisees: "Whenever you give a lunch or dinner, do not invite your friends or brothers or relatives or wealthy neighbors. They might invite you in return and thus repay you. No, when you have a reception, invite beggars and the crippled, the

lame and the blind. You should be pleased that
they cannot repay you, for you will be repaid
in the resurrection of the just."

Jesus asks us to recognize Him in the person
of the poor. In His description of the Last
Judgment, He observes: "I assure you, as often
as you did it for one of my least brothers, you
did it for me." (Matthew 25, 40)

Jesus is the suffering servant; privation, pain
and insult were means to bring about our
salvation. As hard as this may seem, this
attitude must be found in the true Christian.
Christians should share in the cross of Christ in
order that the uplifting of the entire people of
God may be accomplished. The primary law of
the Reign of God is the law of love — of God
and of neighbor. Love sometimes requires
acceptance of pain and privation. This points to
a way of life which includes hardships and
suffering, but which remains joyful because it is
a life of love and loving service. Jesus declared,
"Such is the case with the Son of Man who has
come, not to be served by others but to serve,
to give his own life as a ransom for the many."
(Matthew 20, 27) This philosophy, obviously, is
radically different from that of the hedonist who
would seek his own pleasure and advantage,
even though he injures others in the process.

It is apparent, then, that a Christian should
not seek pain or poverty as goals in themselves.
Pain and poverty are acceptable only if they
become means of bringing blessings, love and
joy into the lives of God's People and drawing
us closer to Christ Our Lord. The Christian life-

style springs from a hierarchy of values. Eternal life is more precious than life in this world. In Jesus' words: "Do not fear those who deprive the body of life but cannot destroy the soul; rather fear him who can destroy both body and soul in Gehenna." (Matthew 10, 28) Spiritual values are to be placed above those which are material. Jesus summarizes this view stating, "Stop worrying, then, over questions like 'What are we to eat, what are we to drink, what are we to wear?' The unbelievers are always running after these things. Your heavenly Father knows all that you need. Seek first his kingship over you, His way of holiness and all these things will be given you besides." (Matthew 6, 31-33) Material possessions and physical pleasures are not in themselves evil. However, they may so occupy our attention that we neglect more precious spiritual and eternal objectives.

There is an element of mystery in this aspect of the Christian life-style. Detachment and suffering are ways of drawing us closer to Christ, who is our only way to the Father, and who is the source of the immense blessing of supernatural life. St. Paul summarizes this mystery stating: "If we have been united with him through likeness to his death, so shall we be through a like resurrection." (Roman 6, 5)

In summary, Jesus by word and example teaches us to use material things in moderation, and to be quick to share them with those who are in need. His mission was first and foremost to the poor and alienated. He lived among them, served their needs, loved them, and never showed condescension toward them. He asks us to have a similar attitude toward all the poor, the suffering, and the alienated, and to serve Him through them.

Chapter V:
Work For A
Better Life

Work is an integral feature of a simple life style. If we are willing to work and to engage in walking, bicycling and other types of useful physical activities, we can greatly enrich our lives, and move toward a simpler way of living.

In Chapter II, I mentioned that through gardening we can produce high quality fruits and vegetables at a low cost.[8] Gardening is also an excellent hobby. A few hours per week in a garden involves us in healthful exercise and a refreshing change of atmosphere. It also brings us into wholesome contact with soil, water, air, sunshine, plants and other natural phenomena.

Those who frequently leave their car in the garage and walk, run or bicycle take a great leap forward to good health; they contribute to the elimination of air pollution, and a less wasteful way of living.

Much of our money is spent for items which we could produce for ourselves if we were more diligent and innovative. Examples include: making and mending our clothing, making simple repairs of home and auto, mowing lawns, shoveling snow, cutting fire wood and cleaning up and beautifying our homes and neighborhoods.

Conversely, much of the disorder and ugliness which plague our nation today stem chiefly from sloth, a failure to exert a rational, caring influence on our surroundings. Slums are manmade, the result of a tragic vicious circle. Ugly surroundings erode peoples' concern for order and beauty; such persons further the deterioration of their surroundings. If a slum-dweller sees a broken window, he feels the urge to break other windows; if he sees garbage on the street, he litters that street with more garbage; if he comes upon a defaced building, he is apt to add even more obscene graffiti to that building. We must break this vicious circle. One of the keys to the needed turn-about is the work of concerned, caring individuals as they replace disorder with order, ugliness with beauty.

Not only does work bring beauty, order and useful products into our lives; it is in addition a rewarding exercise of our talents. As we expand our working habits, we become more creative, more skillful, more fulfilled and truly human. A person who seldom works usually has a low esteem of himself, his talents and his accomplishments.

Work becomes still more rewarding when shared with friends. Possible rewarding group work projects might include such things as neighborhood cleanup projects, tree planting, building, remodeling and repairing homes, community gardening, washing and waxing autos, decorating recreational halls, parks and other public gathering places.

A hobby is work which is pursued more for

the satisfaction of the activity than for the product which results. Concern for the esthetic value of an activity is even more evident in such cultural pursuits as painting, music, dancing, drama, and other activities which enrich our lives and the lives of those around us. All such activities have a proper place in a rational way of living. We should seek satisfactions and joys from these activities, where they may easily be found. Not only the practical and useful objective, but also that which is true, good and beautiful, is deserving of our efforts.

Chapter VI:
Community Efforts Toward
Simple Living

To live in isolation from one's neighbors impoverishes everyone concerned. The resulting lack of companionship often prompts people to spend excessively on recreation, alcoholic drinks and other material substitutes for truly human activities. Those who do not cooperate with their neighbors also lose one of the most positive means offered us for the simplification of life styles. Many progams for reducing energy use, for curtailing pollution, for fighting inflation and for enriching life materially and spiritually, can best be pursued on a community-wide basis.

One good example: community gardens are springing up in all parts of the nation. Most urban dwellers lack access to garden plots where the soil, the availability of sunshine and water are suitable for growing fruits and vegetables. These requirements for effective gardening can be met more easily if several families work together, buy or rent a plot of land, arrange for its being plowed each spring, test soil and add appropriate fertilizers, install a water supply and build fences as needed. In some instances these community gardens are operated as cooperatives; some are managed by parishes or other private organizations. Many gardeners produce more fruits and vegetables than their families can consume at peak seasons. A sense of stewardship dictates that surpluses should be preserved rather than wasted. But a practical problem arises; home-canning consumes so much energy and time that it is not economically practical.

The solution to this dilemma is cooperative canning. An outstanding illustration can be found in Berryville, Arkansas. The Rural Producers Cooperative and Community Cannery was begun in 1976. Presently 300 Carroll County families are involved in this cooperative cannery. The fee for joining the cannery is $5.00 per family, or four hours of volunteer work. The cooperative saves members money by purchasing in volume lots jars, sugar and other items needed for canning. Members of the co-op help one another grow the vegetables and fruits to be canned. If they wish to can produce not available in their gardens, the co-op helps them purchase such items at a reasonable cost.

The cannery equipment was purchased with a small CETA grant and from membership dues. The cooperative manager is Craig Fuller, who was hired originally under CETA and who has worked much of the time as an unpaid volunteer. Other communities in Arkansas and throughout the nation are beginning to establish cooperative canneries using the Berryville plan as their model.

And of course there are other illustrations of community-based programs for simple living. In

Winona, Minnesota, for example, a plan is being developed for more efficient energy use. It is the goal of the people of Winona to become energy self-sufficient by the year 2000 through a three-phase process: a) conservation; b) use of alternative, locally available energy sources; and c) turning to labor-intensive rather than energy-intensive social patterns.

The city of Hartford, Connecticut has completed a study considering the establishment of an alternative urban food system. Components of this system might include: children employed with CETA funds to grow food for low-income populations; an increase in community gardens, using the communities' wastes as fertilizers; widespread adoption of buying clubs, co-ops and farmers' markets; and the organization of community or neighborhood canneries.

In Krebs, Oklahoma, the Nutritional Center is a community cannery which employs twenty-five formerly hard-core unemployed workers and sells produce primarily to local non-profit institutions. Marketing will be expanded to buyers clubs and to a local Choctaw Indian tribe in the near future.

The Bronx, N.Y. Frontier Development Corporation has begun a project which addresses several urgent urban needs, including the problem of an excess of solid wastes and the problem of deteriorating neighborhoods. The corporation has started a large scale composting project which will decrease solid waste disposal costs and contribute to an economic development venture. During June 1978 the first loads of organic wastes were dumped on a 3.7 acre site behind the Hunts Point Sewage Treatment plant. Soon the operation will be turning out over twelve hundred yards of finished compost monthly. The first year's product will be donated to community groups for the development of community gardens and recreational space. Each year thereafter a portion of the compost will be set aside for community use and the rest will be sold to generate revenue.

A neighborhood in Palo Alto, California has proposed the establishment of a neighborhood-based solar utility. A carport will be constructed over the parking lot of a community medical center, solar panels mounted on it, and the hot water generated will be distributed to an entire block. The city-owned utility company is working with neighborhood residents to develop designs and finance mechanisms.

And of course many religious communities have traditionally aimed at simpler life styles. Members of Roman Catholic orders of men and women take a vow of "poverty." Ideally, this means a detachment from material possessions and a moderate use of goods and services. For many centuries men and women who belong to religious orders have been faithful to this vow. Living a community life enables them to share essential property and respond effectively to the spiritual and material needs of the people they serve. Some of these religious communities have embraced poverty to a heroic degree. For example, members of the Madonna House community at Combermere, Ontario, attire themselves with used, donated clothing. The poor whom they serve have first pick of these items, members of the community using whatever is left over. The Little Sisters of the Poor and many Franciscan Sisters provide highly professional care to patients in their hospitals, while they live most frugally in their convents.

On the other hand, some religious communities have acquired very comfortable living quarters and provided themselves with food, clothing and recreation which are more luxurious than their vow of poverty would ideally suggest. Recently, many such religious communities have taken steps to remedy this admitted disorder. They are divesting themselves of non-essential properties and substantially reducing their consumption of goods and services.

Traditional Protestant groups such as Mennonites and Amish combine rural living with a religiously motivated simple life style. They are largely self-sufficient in the food they consume. Most of their clothing is homemade. Their recreations are centered in family and neighborhood. Many still use horse drawn farm machines and buggies. And in recent years new religious organizations have appeared with such simple living as a major goal. Charismatics of the mainline Protestant and Roman Catholic Churches have, for example, been forming a few residential communities in which simple life-styles are beginning to flourish. During August 1973, Faith Village was formed by the Alleluia Community in Augusta, Georgia. This group purchased 36 apartments in one square block in downtown Augusta. Members of the Alleluia Community quickly took up residence in half of these apartments. Each household takes from its income only that amount which is essential; the balance is used for the needs of Faith Village. Members of the Village eat together three times a week and celebrate the Eucharistic Liturgy three times a week.[9]

Larger and more widely-known is the Word of God community in Ann Arbor, Michigan. Begun in 1967 as a charismatic prayer group, 74 living cells — called "households" — have been formed. Eighteen of these consist of the residents in specific corridors of University of Michigan dormitories. They meet frequently for prayer and share some everyday tasks in common. Twenty-three groups live in residential houses in and about Ann Arbor. They share meals, household duties, money and recreations. Eleven of these households pool their incomes and hold their possessions in common. A major part of their way of life is a generous giving of time and money to aid those in need.[10]

The Episcopal Church of the Redeemer in Houston, Texas is an even more impressive example of community living and simple living in response to the Holy Spirit's promptings. Back in 1965, this was a dying church in a decaying neighborhood. Then a new rector and a small group of laymen began to renew the parish. The results have been spectacular. On Sundays its services are full to overflowing. Over 400 of its members have made a total commitment to the ministry of the church, placing their possessions in a common pot, living together in small communities, and laboring and praying together. Since their life style is communal and simple, thirty of their number have been freed to work in a nearby public school and another thirty work in a local health clinic.

It is not yet apparent how significantly the charismatic renewal will affect life styles. Inherent in the charismatic experience is a love for neighbor and trust in divine providence which should move such persons toward a simple life style and a sharing of goods with the poor.

These are, in any case, just a few of the ways in which people of a community, working together, can simplify their life-styles and become better stewards of natural resources in the process. In addition to the economic advantages of such cooperation, the quality of life for the persons involved is significantly increased. Working together for common goals is one of the ways in which we can better fulfill our potential as individuals, and as members of society.

Chapter VII:
The Reign of God

A Christian is called to be a reformer; he views himself as an extension in space and time of Jesus and His "Reign of God." The reign of which Jesus speaks so often and so forcefully implies a new order in society, a new set of values, and new goals. The entire thirteenth chapter of the Gospel according to St. Matthew is a collection of parables which describes the Reign of God. Jesus tells us that He intends to permeate and transform society, the way leaven permeates and lifts up the bread dough; He says that His reign will grow from a tiny beginning, and embrace a very large portion of humanity, just as the mustard seed grows into a very large plant; He tells us that His reign is precious, like the pearl of "great price" or the treasure hidden in the field; and He warns that there will be conflicting forces at work in His reign just as there are weeds growing among the wheat. Jesus indicates that each of His followers must assume responsibilities in His reign. The Parable of the Sower and the Seed relates how different are the ways in which various persons react to God's Word and God's challenges.

A Christian with a vision of God's reign assumes a new attitude toward money and property, toward family and community. Such

a person prizes beauty and utility. Beauty —
because the kingdom must be beautiful, a
reflection of God's goodness and beauty. Utility
— because in the Divine Plan, material things
must serve the needs of man, enrich his life, and
aid him in his pursuit of legitimate goals.

Paul the Apostle in his Epistle to the
Romans (8, 20-21) suggest that, through the sins
of mankind, creation was corrupted; and he
tells us that through redeemed mankind creation
will be uplifted. "Creation was made subject to
futility, not of its own accord but by him who
once subjected it; yet not without hope, because
the world itself will be freed from its slavery to
corruption and share in the glorious freedom of
the children of God."

Many times every day, each of us makes
practical choices which either add to the
corruption of creation, or make it a part of the
Reign of God. Among the latter choices we can
count even such simple actions as picking up
trash and planting flowers; or we can count the
major choices we make regarding the conservation of natural resources, the preservation of
our environment, and the aid we give the poor.
In other words, pursuing a simple life-style is a
major feature of our role in establishing the
Reign of God.

A person with this perspective will refuse to
make material things ends in themselves, or to
abuse them. On the other hand, such a perspective strongly motivates one to treasure creation
as an integral part of the Reign of God, a part
of the new order He is striving to establish.

A visit to a city slum will provide much evidence of how mankind corrupts creation. (Let us put aside for the moment our own responsibility for the social conditions which cause these ghettoes.) Broken glass, garbage, unpainted houses, unkept lawns — all are ugly and all manifest mankind's irresposible acts. On the other hand, driving through the midwest on a summer day, one can see countless farms which are well-groomed and most attractive. The corn, oats, bean and wheat fields are lush, indicating that God's gift of fertility and productivity has been enhanced by man's use of hybrid seeds and fertilizers. The handsome, painted and well-landscaped farm buildings are orderly and an embellishment to the natural beauty of the countryside. The Christian, enlightened by revelation and uplifted by redemptive grace, should not only preserve but also enhance the beauty and productivity of creation. He should make his surroundings both a sign of and a reward for responsible and truly human living.

It is most particularly in our attitude to our neighbor that we see our values in perspective. Are children loved and nurtured? Are young people given responsibility and discipline? And are the aged supported and respected? To the extent that we help establish the Reign of God, human needs will be met, human suffering will be abated and human dignity will be enriched.

Every Christian who resolves to help establish the Reign of God will live simply but purposefully. He will not abuse creation, but on the other hand he will derive much joy from the proper and positive use of God's gifts. The Incarnation sets the tone for Christian living. The Christian does not reject the ideals of humanity; he does not disdain good and beautiful things. Rather he labors to make all these things a part of something more wonderful, a Reign of God in which all of mankind experience justice and joy. Such a person rejects the excessive and abusive use of material things precisely because he is called to use these things in orderly fashion and for a higher purpose.

Chapter VIII:
The Beatitudes,
Eight Ways To Happiness

I n Chapter VI we noted that Jesus urges moderate use of material things, urges us to love the poor, and to give service to God through service to the poor. In the Beatitudes He goes much further. He tells us to put our trust completely in God and to be quite indifferent to the world's wisdom, power and possessions. This gives a very firm foundation for a simple, Christian life-style.

In the Beatitudes, Jesus offers a formula for happiness in this world and complete happiness in the next. The Beatitudes serve as a prologue to the Sermon on the Mount which in turn presents the charter for His Reign. In other words, the Beatitudes are an extremely succinct reflection of the gospel message and of Jesus' religous philosophy.

The basic fact underlying the Beatitudes is that we are God's little ones. We are poor and powerless precisely because we follow God's way, rather than attempt to please the world's powers. This theme is found frequently in the Old Testament. Old Testament writers refer to the "anawim," the little ones, who are faithful to God at all costs. For example, we hear the Lord declare in the prophecy of Zephaniah (3, 12) "But I will leave as a remnant in your midst a people humble and lowly who shall take refuge in the name of the Lord." We read in the 115th Psalm (Verse 11) "Those who fear the Lord trust in the Lord; He is their helper and their shield."

In the Beatitudes we are urged to trust completely in divine justice. We should cast our lot with God and know that eventually His justice will surely prevail. Mercy is urged precisely because it is a manifestation of love to those who are most in need of our care. The "clean of heart" are pure in mind, emotion and action. There is no evil in such a person's intentions or overt actions. Peacemakers are also declared happy because the promotion of peace is basic to the mission of Christ and His Reign.

The rewards for those who observe these counsels are happiness in this world and complete happiness in the next. However, specific implications of this reward are expressed in each of the Beatitudes. "The reign of God is theirs," indicates that such persons truly belong to the Church and to Christ's Reign. With such membership will come special rewards and blessings. "They shall inherit the land, "reflects the Jews' great attachment to the land as a source of security and a symbol of God's fidelity to His promises and His care. "They shall see God," admits of several interpretations. Even in this life through grace and the gifts of the Holy Spirit we are able to know God intimately. Seeing God will reach a perfect stage through the beatific vision in heaven. Those who observe the Beatitudes are called "Sons of God." Through grace we become brothers and sisters of Christ and truly Sons of God. This is indeed one of the greatest of our rewards.

Not only does Jesus teach through the Beatitudes, His life is a perfect exemplification of them. Jesus is humble and gentle. He is the suffering servant. Jesus is merciful and quick to forgive. He is truly the greatest champion of peace. Yet Jesus is joyful, strong, and unafraid. We find in His life a furhter indication of the kind of reward which awaits those who observe the Beatitudes.

St. Paul reaffirms the theme of the Beatitudes in his first letter to the Corinthians (1, 26-29) "Not many of you are wise, as men account wisdom; not many are influential; and surely not many are well-born. God chose those whom the world considers absurd to shame the wise; He singled out the weak of this world to shame the strong. He choose the world's low-born and despised, those who count for nothing, to reduce to nothing those who are something; so that mankind can do no boasting before God."

In the Beatitudes Jesus challenges us to acknowledge a basic fact: that we are very little in comparison to God. God's wisdom, power, and goodness far exceed ours. We are urged to unite ourselves with Him and to align our lives and life's ambition with His. In this way His power, love, and strength will work through us and bring us happiness and security.

A Christian, therefore, is called to be

different from wordly people. Instead of preoccupying ourselves with material goods, pleasure, wordly ambitions, and all the rest, we are urged to trust in God and to look forward to the ultimate triumph of God, His justice, and His ways.

The ultimate reward of God's little ones is eternal happiness in heaven. There God will "wipe every tear from their eyes, and there shall be no more death or mourning, crying out or pain, for the former world has passed away." (Revelation 21, 4) Then the prophecy contained in the Magnificat will be fulfilled: "He has deposed the mighty from their thrones and raised the lowly to high places. The hungry He has given every good thing, while the rich He has sent empty away." (Luke 1, 52-53) A follower of Jesus obviously has more reason than anyone else to embrace a simple life style. This Christian life-style will perhaps seem absurd to a good many wordly people. However, in light of the truths of revelation, such a life style brings the Christian into a more intimate union with Christ and His Heavenly Father, and opens to the Christian the only true happiness and security.

Chapter IX:
St. Francis Embraced Poverty; Found Freedom And Joy

The name of St. Francis of Assisi is almost synonymous with the notion of a simple, joyful way of life. Francis is known and loved by millions as the "Little Poor Man of Assisi." The more he embraced poverty, the greater the freedom and joy he experienced.

St. Francis was born and baptized Giovanni Bernardone at about the year 1182. ("Francis" — "the Frenchman" — was a nickname given him by friends later because his father was on a business trip to France when Giovanni was born.) His father was a prosperous cloth merchant. As a young man Francis enjoyed the luxury and pleasures which wealth made possible. Although he was bright, he did not apply himself diligently to his studies; he was too much of a free spirit to take studies or work seriously.

At the age of 20, during one of the inter-city wars which prevailed in twelfth century Italy, Francis was captured by the Perugians and held in prison for a year. During that time, he also fell seriously ill. This experience of imprisonment and illness brought a degree of maturity into Francis' life.

After his release, he signed up with Walter de Brienne for a military campaign in Southern Italy. Francis purchased a grand and soldierly outfit, but when he came upon a man in rags, he exchanged his own clothes for the rags. Francis failed to join the campaign to which he had committed himself.

A turning point in Francis' life occurred when he encountered a leper near Assisi. The leper asked for alms, and Francis gave them, but in a rather impersonal manner. After the leper left, Francis regretted his coldness. He sought out the leper and embraced him. Francis began to experience the freedom which he had been seeking for years.

In an effort to raise funds to repair the Church of San Damiano, Francis sold cloth from his father's warehouse. In the conflict with his father which ensued, Francis was dispossessed by his father. He publicly gave back to his father the money derived from the stolen cloth, together with all his clothes. A new degree of freedom was experienced by Francis as a result of detachment from family and possessions.

Francis and a few followers made the needed repairs of San Damiano Church. Thus began the process which resulted in the formation of the Franciscan Order. At Mass one day in 1208, the Gospel lesson was taken from Matthew 10, 7ff: "As you go, make this announcement: 'The reign of God is at hand.' . . . the gift you have received, give as a gift. Provide yourselves with neither gold nor silver nor copper in your belts;

no traveling bag, no change of shirt, no sandals, no walking staff." Francis took these words as the basic rule of his order. He and his brothers embraced poverty because they believed that it was at the root of the Gospel message, the counsel on which the other evangelical counsels depend.

Francis saw the poverty of Jesus and Mary as a powerful motive for his own poverty and that required of his brothers in the order. The first rule of the order contains these words: "Let all brothers strive to follow the humility and poverty of Our Lord Jesus Christ . . . . And let them not be ashamed thereof, but rather remember that Our Lord Jesus Christ, the Son of the living and omnipotent God, was poor, and a stranger, and lived on alms, He Himself, and the Blessed Virgin, and His disciples."[11]

Chapter X:
Mother Teresa, Poverty
for the Sake of Service

St. Francis embraced poverty and thus discovered his mission of preaching and serving. Mother Teresa of Calcutta chose her mission among India's poor, and that mission brought her to poverty.

Mother Teresa is a Superior of a religious order known as The Missionaires of Charity. These Sisters serve the most impoverished, the most abandoned, of the poor in Calcutta and other cities of the world. Mother Teresa and her Sisters are not poor in a strictly monetary sense. The Missionaries of Charity receive large amounts of money and other gifts from generous donors. If they chose, they could live in comfort, or even in luxury. But they deliberately choose a life of rigorous poverty, directing almost all of their resources to the needs of their clients rather than to themselves. Mother Teresa further explains their motives: "We would not be able to understand and effectively help those who lack all, if we do not live like them.[13] Moreover, "We must free ourselves to be filled with God. Even God cannot fill what is full."

Mother Teresa was born on August 27, 1910 of Albanian parents at Skopje, Yugoslavia. Her baptismal name was Agnes Gonxha Bejaxhiu.

While Agnes was a high school girl, she learned from a Yugoslav Jesuit working in the Calcutta Archdiocese of the great challenge of missionary work in India. She volunteered to serve in the Bengal Indian mission. With this objective in view, she joined the Loreto Nuns in Ireland who were working in the Calcutta Archdiocese. She took the religious name, Sister Teresa. From 1929 through 1948 she taught geography at St. Mary's High School in Calcutta. While there she learned of the great poverty of the "street people" of Calcutta. These are people who live and die in the streets, and experience unbelievable poverty and deprivation.

During January 1948, Sister Teresa requested permission from her superior to live outside the cloister and to work in the Calcutta slums. In December of that year she opened her first slum school in Moti Jheel. At about the same time she also became an Indian citizen. In October 1950, the new Congregation of the Missionaires of Charity was approved by the Holy See. Sister Teresa became Mother Teresa, the Superior of the Order. Novices for the Order came in great numbers; as of 1976 there were a total of 935 professed Sisters. In 1973 a male counterpart to the Sisters' Order was created, and there are now nearly 200 Brothers in the community. The institutions and works of the Order have likewise expanded phenomenally. By 1976, these included thirty-two homes for dying and destitute people, twenty-eight homes for abandoned children, sixty-seven leprosy clinics, and three hundred thirty-five mobile dispensaries. Presently the Missionaries of Charity are feeding millions of hungry people and caring for over 43,000 lepers.

Mother Teresa has much in common with St. Francis. Both found their chief motive for serving the poor in seeing and serving Christ in those who are most impoverished. Mother Teresa has repeatedly stated that in the poor she and her Sisters encounter Christ "in His most distressing disguise." A few excerpts from her counsels to Sisters of the Order throw further light on this issue: "I believe in person to person; every person is Christ for me, and since there is only one Jesus, that person is the one person in the world at the moment."[14] The goal is not only to provide food and other material necessities; more important is the gift of love and the removal of loneliness. "God has identified Himself with the hungry, the sick, the naked, and homeless; hunger, not only for bread, but for love, for care, to be somebody to someone; nakedness, not of clothing only, but nakedness of that compassion that very few people give to the unknown. Homeless, not only just for a shelter made of stone, but that homelessness that comes from having no one to call your own."[15]

Mother Teresa frequently stresses the parallel between recognizing Christ in the Holy Eucharist and seeing Him in the poor: "If we can see Jesus in the appearance of bread, she says, "we can see Him in the broken bodies of the poor."[16]

One of the chief missions of the Missionaries

of Charity is to provide care to those who are so ill and destitute that death seems inevitable. Mother Teresa explains this feature of their service as follows: "We help the poor die with God."[17]

Mother Teresa sees the obvious parallel between their calling and that of Jesus: "A living love hurts. Jesus, to prove His love for us, died on the cross. The mother, to give birth to her child, has to suffer; if we really love one another properly, there must be sacrifice."[18]

Mother Teresa urges her Sisters not only to care for the poor, but to do so lovingly and with joy: "Keep giving Jesus to your people, not by words, but by your example, by your being in love with Jesus,, by radiating His holiness and spreading His program of love everywhere you go."[19] No Missionary of Charity is permitted to assist the poor on the streets if she is acting sad or depressed. According to Mother Teresa, such sadness is a betrayal of the very ideal which their mission emobodies.

Mother Teresa is sometimes criticized for her lack of interest in long-range development programs which might strike at the root of poverty. Some say that she should be more involved in political activities which might correct some of the systemic disorders which impoverish people. To her critics Mother Teresa responds: "I am called to help the individual, to love each poor person, not to deal with institutions."[20] She adds that, while the efforts of her Order are insignificant in comparison to the problem, still they are important: "We ourselves feel that what we are doing is just a drop in the ocean. But if that drop was not in the ocean, I think the ocean would be less because of that missing drop."[21]

Most Christians will ask themselves whether the arduous life of Mother Teresa and her Sisters is in any way applicable to their own way of life. The answer to this is that every Christian is certainly called to see, love and serve Christ in the poor. No one can rightfully be neglectful of the needs of the poor for food, clothing, shelter and love. The chief difference between the Missionaries of Charity and the average individual is that the former have a special Christian calling. They embrace not only the minimum demands of Christianity but also follow Christ's counsels in a special way. Mother Teresa strongly insists that her sort of service to the extremely poor is a special vocation.

Obviously, the voluntary poverty of Mother Teresa and St. Francis differs in degree from the simple life-style recommended in previous chapters, but the ways of life are connected in that they ask us to redirect our resources to the poor, and substitute a spiritual attitude for a materialistic one. St. Francis and Mother Teresa exemplify in an eminent way the ideals to which I am pointing.

Chapter XI:
Americans Who Live Simply

St. Francis and Mother Teresa are illustrations of austere and heroic poverty. They seem remote from our surroundings and our culture. However, it would be erroneous to conclude that contemporary Americans are incapable of or uninterested in a simple life style. All over our nation, people from every walk of life are adopting more modest habits of consumption. The following are a few examples, some drawn from my own diocese (which for obvious reasons I know best), and others from farther away.

One good example is Bishop Bernard J. Topel of Spokane, Washington. Bishop Topel has moved toward an increasingly austere way of life during the past decade. His participation in Vatican Council II prompted him to adopt a simple manner of living. He wrote in his diocesan newspaper, the *Inland Register:* "During the Council, bishops often spoke of the Church as the Church of the poor. This troubled me because I do not see that we are. . . .

"What has been wrong, I am convinced, is that those of us who should be giving leadership in following Christ's teaching have not been living the message of Christ the way we should be living it. We water it down. The salt has lost its savor."[22]

Bishop Topel proceeded to sell his episcopal mansion and give the money to the poor. He moved into a small four-room house in a low-income neighborhood of Spokane. He also sold his episcopal cross, ring and croizer, using the proceeds to assist the poor. For many years he has collected no salary, living on the $140 per month which he receives from social security. He supplements his income by tending a sizeable garden which provides vegetables for himself and for some of his neighbors. During the past ten years he has purchased almost no clothing for himself.

During 1977, when the nation became more conscious of the energy crisis, Bishop Topel responded by reducing the winter temperature in his little house to the middle forties. During sub-zero weather, he keeps himself warm by wearing several pairs of socks, an old overcoat, a hat, a scarf, and, if need be, galoshes.

The spirit of poverty makes Bishop Topel both more sensitive to, and better able to respond to, the needs of the people of his diocese, particularly the poor. A Catholic school education is available to most families in the diocese. The diocese is also served by a modern retreat house, a college seminary, two homes for unwed mothers, a home for homeless women, a hostel for transient men, a ranch for problem boys, five apartment complexes for the elderly, and a convalescent home for the aged. For twenty years the Spokane Diocese has staffed and supported a mission among the Quiche Indians of Guatemala.

If you ask Bishop Topel why he adopted such an austere way of life, he will quickly reply that it is a result of his prayer life. In prayer it became clear to him that God wanted this of him.

As a Christian draws closer to God, he becomes more detached from the world's goods. Conversely, the more detached we are the more easily we communicate with God in prayer. As our prayer life progresses, we become more sensitive to the needs of the poor.

By word and example Bishop Topel urges the affluent of his diocese to examine their life-style and to be more generous to the missions and to the poor. At the same time, he admonishes the poor to be grateful to God for their poverty, and to offer it up to Him as an act of love.

Rearing a large family on a modest income makes a simple life style both advisable and possible. Advisable — because extravagance in such a family would lead to bankruptcy. Possible — because in a large family there are many joys which are in no way related to the spending of money.

Consider, for example, Fred and Colette Rogers of Edelstein, Illinois and their four sons and four daughters. Back in 1959, after three of their sons and three of their daughters had been born, Fred accepted a position as a civil engineer for Peoria County. He decided to supplement his income by purchasing a twenty acre farm near Edelstein, Illinois. He and his older sons completely remodeled the eight room house located on the farm. On most of the acreage the Rogers family grows corn and soybeans, with ample space reserved for a vegetable garden and a recreational field. The garden greatly reduces food costs, especially since Colette has always canned much of the produce. Clothing costs are kept manageable by Colette's making new clothes and altering "hand-me-downs." As the children reached the teen-age years, they made the Rogers home their favorite recreational facility. Several members of the family play musical instruments including guitars, piano and trumpet. Songfests, cards and other games provide recreation not only for the Rogers family but for a large number of their friends. Family prayers, painting, and home decorating are among the positive ways in which the Rogers family spend their time together.

A family living out in the country must have transportation. The cost of transportation has been significantly reduced by the purchase of second-hand cars, which for the most part Fred services and repairs. When the children were old enough, they sought jobs in nearby communities and quickly became less dependent upon their parents for their financial needs.

During one six-month period of 1978, two daughters and two sons of the family were married. Fred and Colette provided appropriate church weddings for each of their children, while keeping the costs at a very modest level. This was accomplished partly by the girls' making dresses for their attendants and calling upon neighbors to assist with the wedding receptions.

One of the tests of a simple life style is whether it results in a happy and fulfilling life. Anyone who visits the Rogers family, as I have, can have no doubt that they are happy people.

Seldom have so many lived so simply for so long a time. I refer to the officers and volunteers of the United Farm Workers during their long struggle to unionize the agricultural industry. Their life style was simple of necessity; they lacked the financial resources to pay themselves anything more than subsistence wages. Conversely, the willingness of U.F.W. people to live extremely simply isolated them to a large extent from the severe pressures mounted against them by growers, the Teamsters, the police, and politicans. The ultimate victory of U.F.W. in this struggle was a classic illustration of the power of non-violent but resolute people. Back in 1972, U.F.W. President Caesar Chavez established the union's headquarters at an abandoned tuberculosis sanitarium thirty miles east of Bakersfield, in Keene, California. Chavez renamed the place "La Paz", which means "Peace." Here Chavez, his wife and three of his eight children, officers of U.F.W. and about 180 U.F.W. volunteers live a very simple community life. Each of them, including Chavez himself receives $5.00 per week wages plus expenses. They take most of their meals at the La Paz community dining hall.

Caesar Chavez is a vegetarian, and on two occasions he observed twenty-five day fasts. The motive for his fasting was partly religious, and partly a reflection of his own firm inclination toward simple living.

The United Farm Workers is not merely a union; it is "La Causa." A part of the cause for which Chavez and his associates are striving is a more truly dignified way of life for the Mexican-American people whom he represents. At least in its initial stages," La Causa" requires of its members an extremely simple life style.

Farmers affect environment and influence the consumption of energy and other natural resources by their farming methods as well as by their life-styles. Each farmer must choose between large acreage with high capital investments, or relatively small farms with labor intensive production.

Roy and Pat Seipel of Maryville, Missouri, opted for the latter type of agriculture. They have managed to rear a family of seven children in frugal comfort on a 120-acre farm. They decided many years ago that through dairying they could make more responsible use of their land resources and of their own labor and that of their children. They milk twenty-five cows. They also grow a large garden, observing organic farming methods (that is, they use no chemical fertilizers, pesticides or herbicides). When they purchased their farm twenty-one years ago, the Seipels made their old six-room house more comfortable by adding an indoor bathroom. Humble as it is, this house has been the chief focus of family living, praying, recreation and much of their labor. Mrs. Seipel sews and repairs much of the clothing worn by the family.

Roy and the boys add to family income by digging graves and mowing grass at the parish cemetery. Since Roy spent four years in the Navy as a mechanic, he is able to repair his own farm machinery. The family butchers beef for its own use, and they sell some dressed beef to others.

There has never been a televison set in the Seipel home. At first, the reason was because they could not afford to purchase it; now because they want more time for family prayer, homework, reading, and music.

The Seipels are active in church and community affairs. Mrs. Seipel is active in the Diocesan Council of Catholic Women and has served for six years on the Board of Directors of the National Catholic Rural Life Conference. One of the girls of the family, Patricia, twenty-five, plays the organ at the parish church and participated for two years in the Diocesan Volunteer Teaching Program. She has recently taken up residence in a prayer community called "Our Father's House" in Kansas City, Missouri. Tom, twenty-one, teaches religion classes at St. Gregory's Parish. A desire to be of service to the church prompted Roy to seek ordination as a Permanent Deacon, which significantly increased the effectiveness of his service in his parish and diocese.

In spite of their very limited income, the Seipels have provided a Catholic education for their children. The children have worked hard for loans, grants and scholarships. Kenneth, twenty-six, graduated from St. Joseph's College, Rensselaer, Ind.; his twin, Kathleen, is a graduate of Marymount College, Salina, Ks.; Patricia graduated from Avila College in Kansas City; and Tom, twenty-one, will complete his college studies in the fall of 1978.

When Roy and Pat Seipel go to their eternal reward they will have taken very little from their environment or from society. They will leave behind them a 120-acre farm in better condition and more fertile than it was when they purchased it more than twenty years ago. Most importantly, they will bequeath to Church and society a fine family of young men and women schooled in the ideals of the Christian faith, sensitive to the responsible stewardship of natural resources and willing to serve family, Church and community.

The chief motive for pursuing a simple life-style is love — love for mankind in general, love for the poor or love for children. For James and Mary Frances Peeples of Peoria, the motive is love for children — that is, for their twelve adopted sons and daughters.

James Jr., was adopted by James and Mary Frances thirty-one years ago when it became apparent they would have no children of their own. During the three decades that followed, they adopted four more sons and seven additional daughters. The youngest of these, John, is seven years old. Three of the Peeples' children, Martin, Therese and Rose Marie, are now eighteen. Any visit to the Peeples' home will make it clear that James and Mary Frances truly live for their children. They point with pride to the Master's Degree in Sociology which James Jr. earned at Catholic University of America.

They are also full of admiration for the courage of Susan who has been confined to a wheelchair since an auto accident. Susan is now a junior supervisor at Illinois Bell Telephone Co., Peoria.

The Peeples applaud the concern several of their children have for meaningful social action. Lester, served for three years the troubled teenagers at Guardian Angel Home. Twenty-one year old Mary Anne recently quit her job with the Telephone Company to accept a position at a local child-care home. The entire family is delighted with the extraordinary skill Rose Marie shows as a basketball player. She is an outstanding student at the Academy/Spalding Institute in Peoria; her presence on the girls' basketball team assures another successful season at that high school.

James and Mary Frances must carefully budget both their time and money to meet the essential needs of their family. Mary Frances emphasizes the word "essential." They have set priorities for the use of their time and income, and they let non-essentials go. As the older children advance in years, they provide much of the care needed by the little ones. When the family is at church or downtown, a sort of "buddy system" prevails; each youngster is looked after by an older brother or sister.

James was the first black to become a machinist apprentice for Caterpillar Tractor Company back in 1942. In 1950 he discontinued work at Caterpillar in order to open his own cleaning establishment. Since becoming City Director of Human Relations in 1969, James has greatly reduced his involvement in his cleaning business; however, he intends to resume that business full-time when he retires from city employment.

Mary Frances devoted her time completely to her family until 1975 when little John started kindergarten. Now she works at Cabrini Home, an institution for unwed mothers.

The Peeples family lives in a modest two-story frame house in the near Southside of Peoria. Although this is what some people would call a declining neighborhood, James and Mary Frances maintain that they have had no security problems and have only the best of relations with their neighbors. In order to keep down the cost of food, Mary Frances and the children shop very carefully at supermarkets, noting what items are on sale each day.

Looking back over these last thirty-one years James observes, "If I had it to do over again, I would not change any of our priorities." Mary Frances is convinced that adopting these twelve children was a most happy choice; she is convinced that she and James have been building a family that will be a treasure long after all material possessions have passed away.

Nancy Cole of Barwick, Ky., experienced many years of cruel poverty. Yet, when her own financial situation improved, she gave generously of her time and resources to families even poorer than her own.

In 1948, Nancy's husband lost his life in a fire in the coal mines, leaving her with five children, ranging in age from two months to ten years. After the $4,000 paid by Workmen's Compensation was spent, she supported her large family on a $112 per month Social Security check. To make ends meet, she planted a garden, canned much of the produce and raised a few pigs, chickens and one milk cow. She made most of the family's clothing and purchased the rest from second-hand stores.

Nancy's income improved somewhat in 1965 when she was hired as an outreach worker by the Appalachian Volunteers. She accepted a similar position with Grass Roots Economic Development Corporation, Jackson, Ky., in 1969 and with the Middle Kentucky Area Development Council in 1972. Since 1977 she has been unemployed.

Countless neighbors have profited from Nancy's leadership and help. She organized a community garden in Barwick, and now sixty-eight families participate in this joint effort. She shared needle-craft skills and organizational know-how with many members of local handicraft co-ops.

Hope for a better future is at last beginning to surface in the mountains of Eastern Kentucky. One of the causes of this hope is certainly the simple life style, the leadership and the generosity of Nancy Cole. In the gospel according to St. Mark Jesus observed a widow who put small copper coins into the temple's collection box. He said to his disciples: "I want you to observe that this poor widow contributed more than all the others who donated to the treasury. They gave from their surplus wealth, but she gave from her want, all that she had to live on." By this measure, Nancy Cole has given with extreme generosity to the people, especially the poor people, of her community.

Those who choose to live as single persons can also contribute significantly to the needs of others and often embrace the simple life style to further their giving. Consider, for example, two single sisters who live in a deteriorating neighborhood of an Illinois city. Although they never raised a family of their own, one taught children in local schools for forty-five years, and the other served nearly an equal number of years as a nurse. They wear the simplest of clothing and live in an extremely modest home. This enables them to give most generously to many worthy charities.

These sisters were taught simple living by their parents, who reared their family on an Illinois farm. As they approached middle age the sisters, in response to the suggestion and the example of Dorthy Day and the Catholic Worker movement, resolved to embrace voluntary poverty. During the past thirty years they have found themselves more and more committed to a life of voluntary poverty, and to sharing what they have with others. As they explain it: "You give to God; He in return gives you much more; you are challenged to give more, but you never can catch up with God's generosity." It is obvious to anyone who visits this home that these sisters have found great happiness in their simple living, their giving to various important causes, and their service to the children and ill persons of their area.

Ed and Kathleen Guinan of Washington, D.C., turned to the simple life in order better to understand and to serve the aged, the unemployed and the impoverished people of that city. With their three small children, the Guinans share communal life with six other members of the Community for Creative Non-Violence.

The title of the community tells its mission. When Ed and four colleagues banded together in 1970, their purpose was, insofar as they were able, to remove violence from community and national life. Kathleen joined the community in 1972. She and Ed were married in 1974. By 1978 twenty-five persons joined the community. No one receives a salary, but each member of the community is provided with room and board. In the earlier days they lived in a university surrounding and approached non-violence in an academic manner. But two years later, they realized that they needed more first hand experience in inner-city living. They understood that they should engage in some practical service to the poor. In 1972, they moved into a cluster of houses at 14th and N Street, the heart of the city ghetto. There they opened Zacchaeus Soup Kitchen; each day 400 people are served there. Food for the kitchen is gathered by begging from wholesale grocers, individuals and from numerous churches and, as a result, every week one thousand pounds of meat vegetables, bread and other staples are donated. A local church provides the buildings for the community. Along with the soup kitchen, the community operates a hospitality house for the homeless, a free medical clinic with a volunteer medical staff of 125 and a halfway house for ex-prisoners.

Cash income for the community is derived from a printing company which Ed manages, called "Collective Impressions." It was established primarily to provide on-the-job training for unemployed local residents. The Guinans and their three children also share communal life with six other members of their community. By buying and preparing food together, they have been able to reduce the cost of meals to eight dollars per adult per week. The other adult members of the household help care for Sarah, Timothy and Matthew, the Guinan children.

Transportation for the community is provided by two vehicles, one a Volkswagen which has been driven more than 100,000 miles. The simple clothing of the household is obtained from a free thrift shop, clothing which of course requires a great deal of sewing and alteration.

It seems appropriate to conclude this chapter with this description of a community of people who have banded together to promote non-violence, to pursue a simple life, and to aid the poor.

Chapter XII:
A Plan Of Action

Those individuals and families who wish to simplify their life styles might find the following plan of action helpful. Most people will not move in a single step from an affluent to a simple life style. Many personal habits and peer pressures militate against such an abrupt change. The following three steps may prove most feasible.

Step One: Aim at a five percent reduction in your consumption of goods and services. This can be accomplished rather painlessly and quickly. The following are suggested ways in which you can reach this goal. First of all, heavy cigarette smokers might reduce their cigarette use to one pack a day. This will greatly reduce the health hazards and, of course, the immediate cost of tabacco. If you consume alcoholic beverages, you might resolve to take only wine and/or beer and these only with food. Beverages with a relatively low alcoholic content are less costly than hard liquors. When taken with food, the good effects begin to outweigh the bad effects of such consumption.

It goes without saying that any use of hallucinatory or narcotic drugs is incompatible with a simple life style even in this first stage. People who are afflicted with such habits should look for professional help, as should addicted gamblers. If you gamble for fun, resolve to gamble only with friends; in this way the companionship will help to dignify and humanize the experience. The beneficiaries of your losses will be friends, not the Mafia.

The auto you buy should weigh less and have a better mileage-per-gallon rating than your present auto. A close scrutiny of your auto travel will indicate how many of these trips are probably unnecessary.

Study your clothing budget; try for better quality clothing at modest costs, with less attention to ephemeral fashions, and resolve to buy clothing only during sale days.

Attempt to reduce the consumption of energy in your home by five percent. This will mean lower temperatures during the winter and more judicious use of applicances, including air-conditioners. Try, on a regular basis, to spend some family recreational time together, at home. This will reduce your family's spending on recreation, and will help to strengthen the bonds among family members.

Most people who take this first step are amazed to find how relatively easy it is. The results, in almost every case, include an increase in personal wellbeing and health, and a more truly human outlook upon material things, and our fellow human beings.

Step Two: Now be prepared for a more severe test — namely, a sacrifical life style. Aim at the transfer of twenty percent of your income to various charitable purposes. (There are some concrete suggestions for this in Chapter XIII.) It will be difficult for you to persevere in this step unless you are strongly motivated for religious reasons. A very special closeness to Jesus Christ and a marvelous experience of freedom are among the rewards of this step.

Look to your food consumption; do more home cooking; use fewer prepared foods and take fewer meals at restaurants. You may have the skill to make or repair clothing; you can also economize by wearing clothes until they are truly no longer useful. Laundering is much cheaper than dry cleaning. As often as practical, choose washables when you buy clothes.

Smokers at this stage should simply quit smoking. Such a step is severely painful. It can be made possible by offering up the distress in union with Christ's passion. This is also the stage at which you use less non-prescription drugs. Most cold remedies are ineffectual; many pain killers are unnecessary.

At this stage of simplification of your life style, you should begin, as frequently as possible, to replace auto driving with walking or bicycling. Of course, you will even more severely restrict unnecessary journeys and take steps necessary to arrange appropriate car-pooling. This is also the time to consider moving to a smaller, less expensive house or apartment. A move of this sort may involve moving from the suburbs to the inner city. In many cities today such a move will result in substantial savings and many conveniences. Public transportation is usually available in the inner city. Long drives to and from work are usually eliminated. Rents and the costs of homes are significantly cheaper.

Step three: Your next challenge is to embrace poverty. If you have taken the first two steps and have found your life enriched and liberated, it is probable that you are capable of this third step. Up to this time your changes of life style have only advanced your own physical well-being. Now, with the counsel of a wise spiritual advisor, you may be ready to reduce your material possessions and consumption of goods and services to a poverty level. In order to take this step with positive results, those material possessions and goods which you give up should be replaced by an increase of prayer, more works of love, and more intellectual pursuits. This step could result in a reduction of consumption by fifty percent.

I recommend specifically that at this stage you eliminate all use of alcohol, tobacco, and gambling. You will resort to a very simple diet, consisting largely of grains, milk, food and vegetables. Most of the meat and fish will be taken in casseroles, with meat extenders such as noodles, spaghetti, etc. A word of caution is in place: deliberate malnutrition is not virtuous; a balanced diet is important.

In this third step you will severely curtail travel and purchased recreation. Another warning is appropriate: everyone needs leisure, and there should be the experience of beauty in everyone's life. You may want to give more time to alternate leisure activities such as gardening, creative writing, music, etc.

Many persons at this stage of simplification of their life style begin to purchase much of their clothing from thrift stores. Excellent and useful items of every kind can be obtained at such stores, at amazingly low prices. As indicated in Chapter XI, many families at this stage take up community living with other families. Such a step should be taken only after thorough exploration of its implications. It would be wise to visit at length with persons who have already had such communal living experiences, and to visit one or more such communities.

The experience of the persons described in Chapter XI also indicate that at this stage many individuals and families become deeply involved in services to the poor. This greatly enriches one's personal and spiritual life, and enables the person who has undertaken such a life to see very directly the fruits of a life of poverty. In order to explore thoroughly this last feature of living a life of voluntary poverty, we shall describe in more detail in Chapter XIII the beneficiaries of your simple living and your giving.

Chapter XIII:
Beneficiaries Of Your Giving

I f you embrace a simpler life style and merely hoard the money saved, you have taken only a half-hearted step. Indeed, this policy is so inconsistent that you will probably give it up after a short time. One of the great blessings of a simple life style is the fact that it frees substantial amounts of money, goods and services for aiding others, particularly the poor and the hungry.

As you increase the extent of your charity, be sure also to improve the quality of that charity.

First, do not limit your giving to money and things; be prepared to give yourself, your time and your affection. Mother Teresa of Calcutta strongly emphasizes the poverty of those for whom no one really cares, those who are loved by nobody. There is a rapid increase in our times of hostels for the homeless and impoverished or handicapped persons. One good example is the Catholic Worker movement. The personnel who staff Catholic Worker houses give their attention and their affection in a very direct and personal way to those who are in the greatest need. This is a heroic way of life and presupposes that the parties involved have advanced to Steps Two or Three, both described in Chapter XII. In addition to generosity, those who conduct such hostels must have a great deal of practical wisdom. Some of those who come to your door will be "con artists." Unless you are able to see what their true needs are, you may harm them as much as you help them.

A somewhat less heroic but very valuable giving of oneself can be exercised in countless volunteer programs. In every community there are scores of services extended to the poor, the ill, the handicapped and the aged which could not survive if it were not for volunteer help. There are several organizations which accept volunteers on a full-time basis for programs at home and abroad. ACTION is the chief government-sponsored volunteer program which fits this description. The International Voluntary Services, Washington, D.C., is one of the oldest and most effective of the privately directed volunteer programs.[23]

Contributing to the missions, or volunteering to serve in the missions, is another way in which you can provide such person-to-person service to those most in need. It is interesting to note that an increasing number of missionaries are proving themselves very effective as catalysts for self-help programs in Third World countries.

Generally speaking, self-help projects are preferable to handouts. You do a greater service to those in need if you help train them and make a job available to them, than you do by giving them a little money or enrolling them with a welfare agency. Not only does their job provide income for them; more importantly, it helps them to regain their self-esteem.

There are, of course, instances in which the poor need money, medicine, food, clothing, and other necessities. In these instances we should be sure that we respond to the needs of the poor in a way which will not be demeaning to them. We must always be gentle, affectionate and patient with those who are poor. Anyone who deals with those in need will inevitably encounter some individuals who seem very cold, and even sometimes hostile. It takes a truly great charity to persevere in efforts at self-help and human uplift, in spite of such handicaps and obstacles placed in the way by the persons being aided.

In addition to aiding the poor, the ill and the handicapped, your simple life style will enable you to contribute more generously to other good causes such as needed educational projects, and various efforts aimed at health improvement or community betterment. Once more I counsel that your giving should be not only generous but also wise. There is a vast difference in the effectiveness of various programs which are seeking your support. Among the criteria you should use to evaluate appeals for charity will be an attention to the amount of overhead spent by the organization on fund-raising and administration, the extent to which they are truly responsive to the real needs of the community, and the extent to which the persons aided are involved in the planning and execution of the program.

Most of the programs described above are concerned with individual needs; most of the people aided will be people in your own community. As you advance in living a simple life-style and in generous giving, you will probably become more concerned about broader issues such as the need for systemic change, and the reforms needed in the world order. Poverty is the result not only of individual shortcomings; it is often the result also of evil systems such as racism, economic exploitation, inadequate education, and governmental corruption and inefficiencies. In order to change such damaging systems, group action is required. At least a part of the remedy must be found in improving governmental services. For this reason, honest and conscientious political action is a great service to one's neighbor and one's nation.

As you look to the world order you will find many glaring problems. Very high on this list is the threat of war, and the staggering expenditure of the world's governments on armaments.

Positive steps toward world peace are among the greatest possible contributions an individual or a group can make to the welfare of mankind. Those who live in an affluent nation such as the United States are usually unaware of the extent to which the poverty of Third World countries has resulted from disadvantageous trade relationships and other policies in which our own nation is involved. A conscientious citizen should become aware of these issues and speak out about them.[24] In summary, the prime motive for a simple life style is love — love for God and neighbor. This chapter is an effort to help those who embrace a simple life style to express love in the most practical and effective manner possible.

In this "pilgrim way", love is usually accompanied by pain. It is for that reason that steps two and three described in the previous chapter are usually necessary.

The more advanced forms of giving may be sucessfully embraced with their help.

Chapter XIV:
The How and Why
of a Simple Life Style

How can we bring about a significant trend toward a simple life style? Let us examine the ways. First, we can begin with young people. They are perhaps not quite so fixed in their life style as older people are. They tend to be idealistic, and are often prepared to do the difficult and even the heroic, if good reasons for doing so have been offered.

The dramatic change in agricultural technology which took place during the past four decades is due in large part to such programs as the 4-H Clubs, Future Farmers of America, and vocational agriculture courses. They helped to convince young people of the feasibility and desirability of such changes. Perhaps we could at this point devise similar programs to help young people now know and appreciate the beauty of a simple life-style.

Young people as well as older ones are more impressed by living models of an ideal than by spoken and written words. If many individuals who are frequently before the attention of the nation turn to a simple life style, we can hope for a trend in that direction. This trend will be accentuated if such models are joyful, believable and competent.

Why pursue a simple life style? Let us look at the motives.

No man is an island. We Americans are profoundly influenced by the culture with which we are surrounded. That culture presently pushes us toward a life-style very different from the one described and recommanded in this book. Only strong and positive motives can cause us to embrace a life-style radically different from that of our peers, and give us the strength to persevere in adhering to it.

In Chapter I, I suggested as a prime motive for a simple life style our desire to keep the planet earth habitable, which, of course, means the exercise of a rational stewardship of the earth's resources. In the last analysis, this is an extremely pragmatic motive: truly, the lives we save may be our own, or the lives of future generations. In view of the continued pollution of our environment and the rapid depletion of energy and other strategic resources, man himself is an endangered species. However, since many of the tragic consequences of extravagant living will surface only in the future, an educational program must be launched now. We must present convincingly to the public the complete price tag of such extravagance.

Among the reasons given in Chapter I for a simple life style is the desire to make available more aid to our less fortunate fellowmen. The basic motive for so doing must be love for those neighbors. The Christian's love for his neighbor is rooted in the conviction that he serves Christ in that neighbor. Mother Teresa of Calcutta states that in the destitute, the diseased and the dying she finds Christ "in His most distressing disguise." She and Sisters of her community nurture that life through prayer and sacraments.

If we share extensively with others, it follows necessarily that we will retain fewer goods and services for our own use. We can compensate for this quantitative reduction by acquiring a deeper appreciation of the things we do retain. This can be accomplished by viewing all possessions, not as our own, but as gifts of God. They reflect His beauty and goodness, and they speak to us of His love. It was precisely because he understood this that St. Francis, "the Little Poor Man of Assisi" was so rich, was so amazingly fulfilled. The simplest of God's creatures were dear to him. He spoke of "Brother Sun" and "Sister Moon." The birds and animals were welcomed by him as emissaries of a loving God. The result was a joyful life, all the more amazing because it was nurtured by so few of those things from which most of us seek our satisfactions.

Among the most positive, the most challenging of motives is the realization that we are called to be the *light of the world*. [25] Christ is the primary light. We should mirror to the world His love, truth, beauty and goodness; His goals, His values and His ways.

However, if our way of life departs significantly from that of Christ, the light we present to the world will be muted and distorted. It will be a clouding of Christ's light, the light with which we are expected to shine.

We must repeatedly and honestly reassess our life-style if we wish to mirror faithfully Christ's light to others.

Notes

1. For a critique of bigness as a goal, see E.F. Schumacher's *Small Is Beautiful*, New York, Harper and Row, 1973.
2. See: *Obesity and Its Management* by Denis Craddock, New York, Lorryman, Inc., 1973.
3. See: "The Great American Animal Farm," *Time Magazine*, Dec. 23, 1974. p. 58-59.
4. Schweitzer, Stuart O. & Bryan R. "Smoking and Alcoholic Abuse: A Comparison of their Economic Consequences." New England Journal of Medicine. March 9, 1978. Vol. 298; ÷ 10.
5. So state researchers Berry, Boland, Smart and Kovak in a report prepared for the National Institute on Alcohol Abuse and Alcoholism, April 1978.
6. This, of course, is an estimate. Drug pushers do not report their income to the Internal Revenue Service.
7. This is the estimate of the Justice Department's Commission on Review of the National Policy toward Gambling, March 1978.
8. According to Bruce Stokes, Worldwatch Institute, Washington, D.C., since 1971, families raising food increased by 7 million. They estimate the value of home grown produce at $14 million.

9. Faith Village and other charismatic communities are described in the November 1974 issue of *New Covenant*, Ann Arbor, Mich.

10. For more information about the Word of God Community see *New Covenant*, February 1975.

11. Thomas De Celano. St. Francisci Assisiensis Vita et Miracula, ed. Romae, Desclee, Lefebre et Soc., 1906, In. 57

12. Leclerc, Eloi. Wisdom of the Poverello, Franciscan Herald Press, Chicago, 1961. p. 29.

13. Mother Teresa of Calcutta. *A Gift for God.* New York, Harper & Row, 1975. p. 35.

14. Ibid. p. 44.

15. Ibid. p. 27.

16. Doig, Desmond. *Mother Teresa, Her People and Her Work.* London, Collins, 1976. p. 165.

17. Ibid. p. 161.

18. Mother Teresa of Calcutta. Op. cit., p. 14.

19. Ibid. p. 41.

20. Ibid. p. 46.

21. Ibid. p. 43.

22. "Your Bishop and You," August 30, 1968 issue of the *Inland Register.*

23. ACTION combines under one administration VISTA for programs in the United States and Peace Corps which promotes self help overseas. ACTION's address is: 806 Connecticut Ave., N.W., Washington, D.C. 20525. International Voluntary Services is located at: Suite 605,

1717 Massachusetts Ave., N.W., Washington, D.C., 20036.

24. For more information on a just world order consult American Freedom From Hunger Foundation, 1625 Eye Street, N.W., Suite 719, Washington, D.C. 20006; and League for Economic Assistance and Development, Inc., 390 Plandome Road, Manhasset, N.Y. 11030.

25. Matthew 5, 24.

Bibliography

Clark, Henry. *The Christian Case Against Poverty.* New York, Association Press, 1965.

Cox, Harvey. *The Secular City.* New York, MacMillan, 1965.

Crawley, Gerard M. *Energy.* New York, MacMillan, 1975.

Doig, Desmond. *Mother Teresa: Her People and Her Work.* London, Collins, 1976.

Enthoven, Alain C. & Freeman, A. Myrich. *Pollution, Resources and the Environment.* New York, Norton & Co., 1973.

Felder, Hiliren & Bittle, Berchman. *The Ideals of St. Francis of Assisi.* New York, Benziger, 1925.

Finnerty, Adam Daniel. *No More Plastic Jesus.* Maryknoll, N.Y., Orbis, 1977.

Leclerc, Eloi. *Wisdom of the Poverello.* Chicago, Franciscan Herald Press, 1961.

Longacre, Doris Janzen. *More-With-Less Cookbook.* Scottdale, Pa., Herald Press, 1976.

Marciniak, Ed. *Reviving an Inner City Community.* Chicago, Loyola U., 1977.

Mother Teresa of Calcutta. *A Gift for God.* New York, Harper & Row, 1975.

Niggs, Walter. *Francis of Assisi.* Chicago, Franciscan Herald Press, 1975.

Schmitt, Myles. *Francis of the Crucified.* Milwaukee, Bruce, 1957.

Schumacher, E.F. *Small is Beautiful.* New York, Harper & Row, 1973.

Sider, Ronald J. *Rich Christians in an Age of Hunger.* New York, Paulist, 1974.

Simon, Arthur, *Bread for the World.* New York, Paulist, 1975.

Taylor, David E. (ed.). *99 Ways to a Simple Lifestyle.* Washington, D.D., Center for Science in the Public Interest, 1976.

U.S. Department of Agriculture. *Gardening for Food and Fun.* Yearbook of Agriculture 1977. Washington, D.C., USDA, 1977.